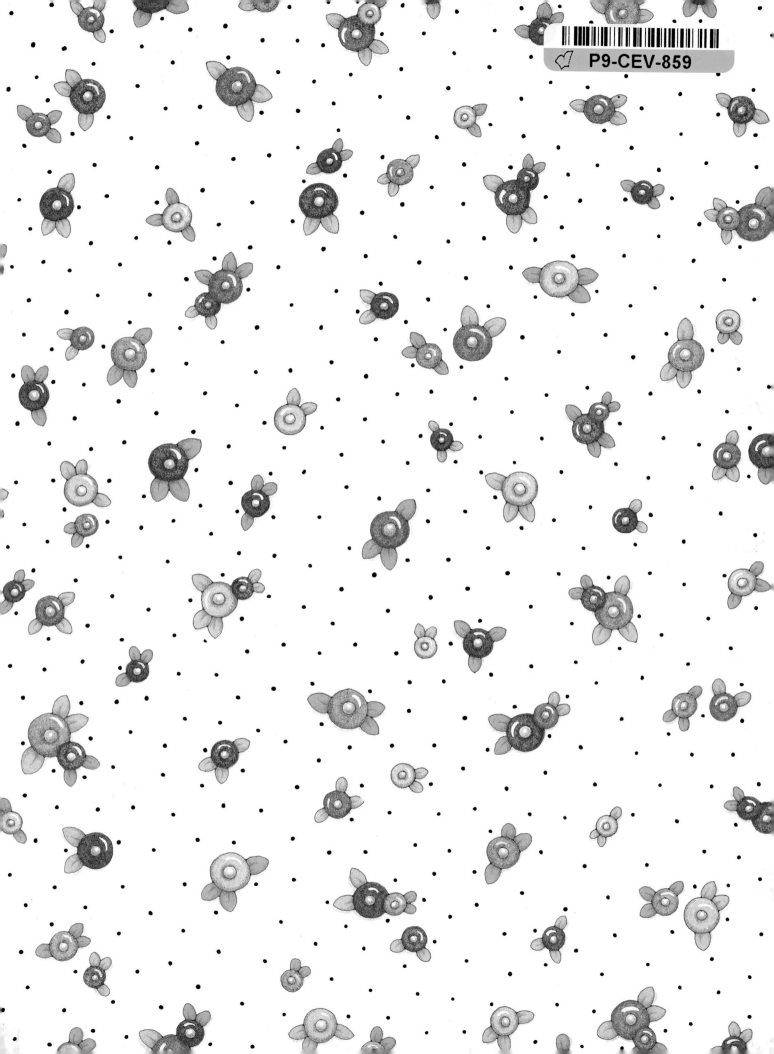

For You . . . With Love.

This journal is my most intimate gift to you.
It is a record of my memories—memories of you
and of many special people who played a part in making you
the unique and wonderful person you are today.

As you read it, I hope you come to know me,
our family, and even yourself more deeply than ever before.

Time has a way of diluting our memories, even those we hold most dear.
Consider this journal your strongest defense. Some of the stories I've included here
will be familiar to you, and others may be a surprise. I hope all of them
give you pleasant memories of your family for many years to come.

This journal is presented to

_____

On the occasion of

_____

Date

_____

With love from

_____

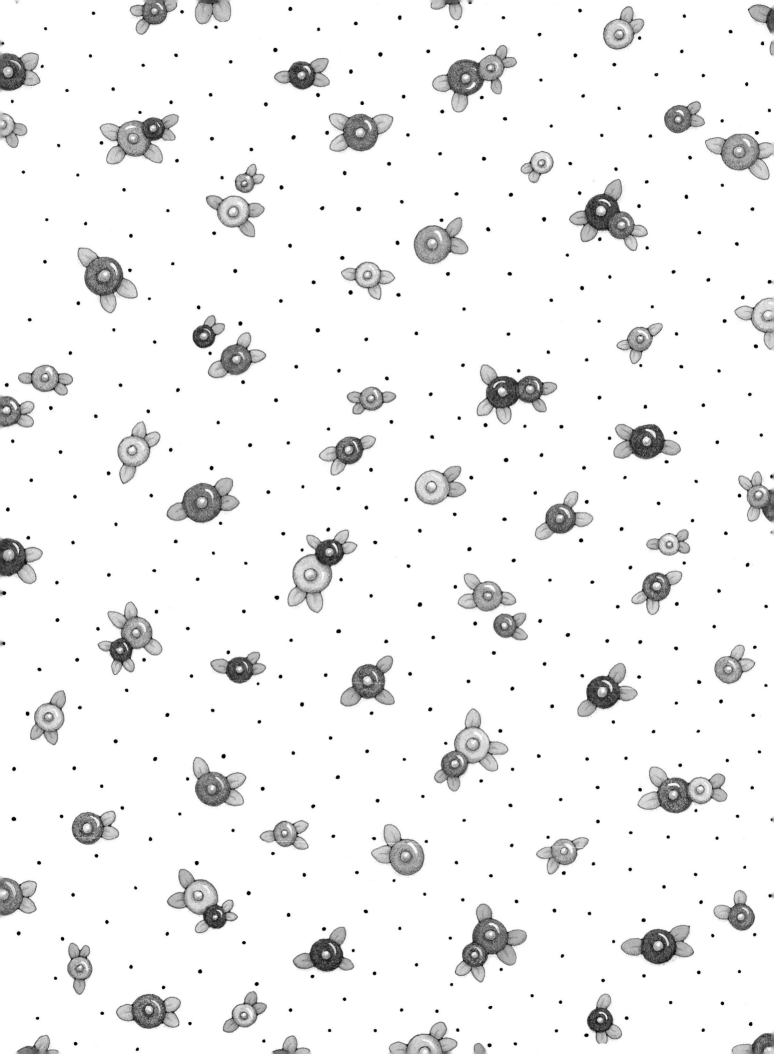

A Mother's Journal
A Collection of Family Memories

Illustrated by Mary Engelbreit
Written by Catherine Hoesterey

Andrews and McMeel
A Universal Press Syndicate Company
Kansas City

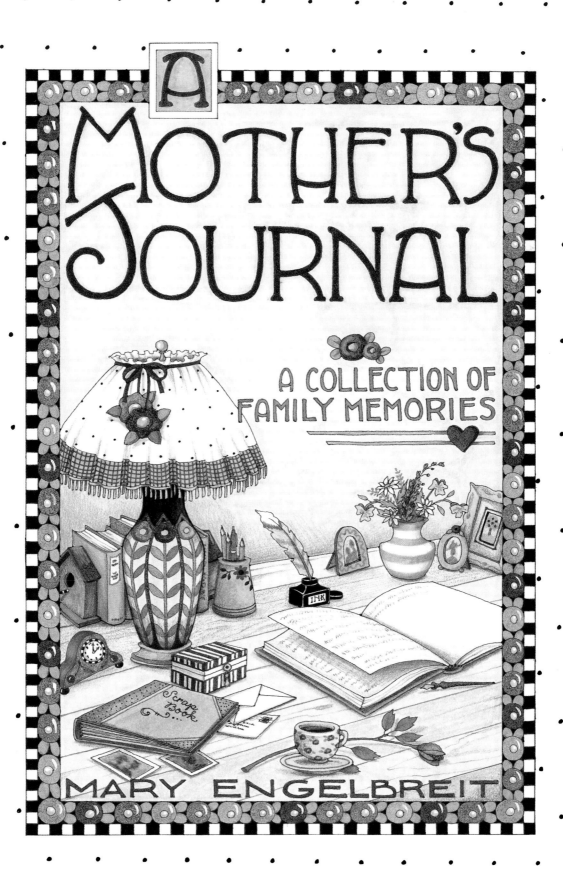

A MOTHER'S JOURNAL

A COLLECTION OF FAMILY MEMORIES

MARY ENGELBREIT

CONTENTS

Family Tree.... 8

Your Great-Grandparents....10

Your Maternal Grandparents....14

Your Paternal Grandparents....17

A Little Bit About Me....21

Growing Up....25

Your Father's Background....26

When I First Met Your Father....28

Our Wedding....30

Our Early Years Together....32

Let's Talk About YOU!....35

The Day You Arrived!....36

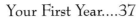
Your First Year....37

From Baby to Pre-school Child....38

Off to School...40

Primary School Years....42

Middle School and Junior High School Years....43

High School Years....44

See How You've Grown!....46

Family Memories....49

Vacations....52

Thoughts I'd Like to Share....55

Let's Start a New Tradition....59

Keepsakes and Remembrances....60

Assorted Thoughts....64

Your Great-Grandparents
Your Mother's Maternal Grandparents

My grandfather's name _____

He was born (place/date) _____

My grandmother's name _____

She was born (place/date) _____

They were married in _____

After marrying, they lived in _____

My grandparents earned their living _____

_____

_____

My strongest memories of my maternal grandparents are _____

_____

_____

_____

_____

_____

_____

An interesting thing about their lives was _____

_____

_____

_____

_____

_____

_____

Your Great-Grandparents
Your Mother's Paternal Grandparents

My grandfather's name _____

He was born (place/date) _____

My grandmother's name _____

She was born (place/date) _____

They were married in _____

After marrying, they lived in _____

My grandparents earned their living _____

_____

_____

My strongest memories of my paternal grandparents are _____

_____

_____

_____

_____

_____

An interesting thing about their lives was _____

_____

_____

_____

_____

_____

Your Great-Grandparents
Your Father's Maternal Grandparents

His grandfather's name _____

He was born (place/date) _____

His grandmother's name _____

She was born (place/date) _____

They were married in _____

After marrying, they lived in _____

His grandparents earned their living _____

_____

_____

A strong memory he has of his maternal grandparents is _____

_____

_____

_____

_____

_____

_____

An interesting thing about their lives was _____

_____

_____

_____

_____

_____

_____

Your Great-Grandparents
Your Father's Paternal Grandparents

His grandfather's name _____

He was born (date/place) _____

His grandmother's name _____

She was born (date/place) _____

They were married in _____

After marrying, they lived in _____

His grandparents earned their living _____

_____

_____

A strong memory he has of his paternal grandparents is _____

_____

_____

_____

_____

_____

_____

An interesting thing about their lives was _____

_____

_____

_____

_____

_____

Your Grandparents
Your Maternal Grandparents

My father's name _____

His brothers and sisters were _____

_____

He was born (place/date)_____

As a young man, he liked to _____

_____

His education_____

_____

He earned his living by _____

_____

_____

His interests and accomplishments included _____

_____

_____

_____

_____

Some of the stories he told me about his childhood _____

_____

_____

_____

_____

_____

My mother's name _____

Her brothers and sisters were _____

_____

She was born (place/date) _____

As a young woman, she liked to _____

_____

Her education _____

_____

She worked as a _____

_____

Her interests and accomplishments included _____

_____

_____

_____

_____

Some of the stories she told me about her childhood _____

_____

_____

_____

_____

_____

_____

WE ARE ALWAYS THE SAME AGE INSIDE

My parents met _____

_____

_____

_____

They were married _____

For their honeymoon, they _____

_____

_____

Their first home was _____

_____

As a young couple they spent a lot of their time _____

_____

_____

_____

_____

Some of my favorite stories about their early years together _____

_____

_____

Your Grandparents
Your Paternal Grandparents

Dad's father's name_____

His brothers and sisters were_____

_____

He was born (place/date)_____

As a young man, he liked to_____

_____

His education_____

_____

He earned his living by_____

_____

_____

His interests and accomplishments included_____

_____

_____

_____

_____

Some of the stories he told about his childhood_____

_____

_____

_____

_____

_____

Dad's mother's name _____

Her brothers and sisters were _____

_____

She was born (place/date) _____

As a young woman, she liked to _____

_____

Her education _____

_____

She worked as a _____

_____

_____

Her interests and accomplishments included _____

_____

_____

_____

_____

Some of the stories she told about her childhood _____

_____

_____

_____

_____

_____

_____

_____

_____

Dad's parents met _____

_____

They were married _____

For their honeymoon, they _____

_____

_____

Their first home was in _____

_____

As a young couple they spent a lot of their time _____

_____

_____

_____

_____

Some of my favorite stories about their early years together ____

_____

_____

_____

_____

AND·THEY·LIVED·HAPPILY·EVER·AFTER

A Little Bit About Me

I was born (date/place) _____

_____

I was named _____ because _____

_____

Other members of my family (in birth order) are _____

_____

As a young child my parents said I was _____

_____

_____

Some of my earliest childhood memories are _____

_____

_____

_____

_____

When I was a child, I thought my parents _____

_____

What holidays were like in my family _____

_____

_____

_____

_____

A description of where we lived _____

_____

_____

_____

A little bit about my siblings _____

_____

_____

_____

Some other relatives who are special to me _____

_____

Games we liked to play as children _____

The clothes we wore _____

_____

As kids, we used to argue about _____

_____

I spent a lot of time _____

_____

_____

_____

Some of my closest childhood friends were _____

_____

_____

_____

_____

What it was like growing up when I was a child _____

_____

_____

When I was child, I dreamed of _____

_____

ONE TOUCH of NATURE MAKES THE WHOLE WORLD KIN

The first person I had a "crush" on _____

_____

_____

As a child I remember being proud of _____

_____

_____

My parents and I could never seem to agree on _____

_____

_____

I once got into a lot of trouble when I _____

_____

_____

_____

My most enduring childhood memory _____

_____

_____

_____

_____

_____

Schools I attended were _____

_____

How school was different compared to schools today _____

_____

_____

In school, I was involved in _____

_____

My best subjects were _____

_____

I started dating when I was _____

On dates, we usually _____

_____

Ways I earned spending money when I was growing up _____

_____

What radio, movies, and television were like then _____

_____

_____

Some national and world events that had an impact on my family and how they affected us _____

_____

_____

_____

_____

_____

_____

Growing up, I worried about _____

_____

_____

Other comments about my childhood _____

_____

_____

_____

_____

_____

_____

Growing Up

After high school, I _____

_____

_____

_____

About college _____

_____

_____

_____

My first job was _____

_____

_____

Something I was proud of during my early adult years was _____

_____

_____

_____

If I could live this part of my life over again, I would _____

_____

_____

The best advice my parents ever gave me was _____

_____

_____

_____

Some not-so-good advice they gave me was _____

_____

Your Father's Background

He was born (place/date) _____

He was named _____ because _____

_____

Other members of his family (in birth order) are _____

_____

A little bit about his siblings _____

_____

_____

_____

Other relatives who are special to him _____

_____

_____

Some of his closest childhood friends were _____

_____

_____

Dad says his most enduring childhood memory is _____

_____

_____

Something you might not know about your father's childhood _____

_____

_____

When your father was a child, he dreamed of _____

Your father says his proudest moment as a child was _____

_____

_____

As a child, your father once got into big trouble for _____

_____

_____

Other comments about his childhood _____

_____

_____

Schools he attended were _____

_____

In school, he was involved in _____

_____

_____

His best subjects were _____

After high school, he _____

_____

About college _____

_____

_____

His first job was _____

_____

Something he was very proud of during his early adult years was _____

_____

_____

When I First Met Your Father

Your father and I first met _____

_____

_____

My first impression of him was _____

_____

_____

He says his first impression of me was _____

_____

_____

What really made him interesting to me was _____

_____

_____

Dad says he was first attracted by my _____

_____

_____

I think we were a good couple because _____

_____

_____

We dated for _____

Things we liked to do together _____

_____

_____

_____

I first thought we might get married when _____

_____

A description of the moment we decided to get married _____

_____

_____

At that time, I was thinking _____

_____

The date of our engagement was _____

In planning the wedding, some of our longest discussions were about _____

_____

_____

My parents' reaction to our engagement was _____

_____

Dad's parents thought _____

_____

Our friends thought _____

_____

_____

_____

_____

_____

_____

_____

_____

_____

Our Wedding

My whole name _____

Your father's whole name _____

Your father and I were married on _____

At _____

The ceremony was performed by _____

The bridal party included _____

_____

_____

_____

_____

Before the wedding, I felt _____

_____

_____

_____

_____

_____

_____

Dad says he felt _____

_____

_____

_____

_____

_____

The wedding reception _____

_____

_____

_____

My strongest memories of our wedding day _____

_____

_____

_____

For our honeymoon we _____

_____

_____

_____

Some additional comments about the wedding _____

_____

_____

_____

_____

_____

_____

O HAPPY DAY!

Our Early Years Together

After we were married, we lived _____
_____
_____
_____
_____

We spent a lot of our time _____
_____
_____
_____
_____

Some of our close friends at that time were _____
_____
_____
_____
_____

During that time, Dad worked at _____
_____
_____
_____

I worked _____
_____
_____
_____

In those early years, we dreamed about _____

_____

_____

_____

_____

We sometimes worried about _____

_____

_____

_____

_____

About our first home _____

_____

_____

_____

_____

_____

_____

_____

Let's Talk About YOU!

When I learned I was pregnant with you, my first reaction was _____
_____
_____
_____

Your father's reaction was _____
_____
_____
_____

Memorable events during pregnancy _____
_____
_____
_____

Names we considered for a boy _____
_____
_____

Names we considered for a girl _____
_____
_____

To prepare for you, we _____
_____
_____
_____

My due date was _____

The Day You Arrived!

Date:_____ Time:_____

Weight:_____ Length:_____

Hair:_____ Eyes:_____

The doctor who delivered you _____

The hospital where you were born _____

We named you _____

We chose this name because _____

_____

When I first saw you, _____

_____

_____

_____

Dad's reaction _____

_____

_____

_____

People said you resembled _____

_____

Those first few days with you _____

_____

_____

_____

_____

_____

...IT IS NOT A SLIGHT THING
WHEN THEY, WHO ARE SO
FRESH FROM GOD,
LOVE US.

Your First Year

In general, as an infant you were _____

_____

Your eating and sleeping habits _____

_____

One thing that would usually make you stop crying _____

_____

A song I used to sing to you _____

You made us laugh by _____

_____

When you started eating food, your favorite was _____

But you didn't like _____

Your favorite toy was _____

Games you liked to play as a baby _____

_____

_____

How other family members acted toward you _____

_____

_____

_____

We celebrated your first birthday by _____

_____

_____

_____

From Baby to Pre-school Child

As a baby, you were cared for primarily by _____

_____

_____

_____

Your first word was _____

You seemed to be fascinated by _____

_____

_____

_____

_____

An object that you became very attached to _____

_____

_____

_____

When you were around other children, you _____

_____

_____

_____

_____

Once you could move around on your own, you loved to _____

_____

_____

_____

_____

One time we were really worried about you as a baby _____

_____

_____

_____

_____

At bedtime, you _____

_____

_____

_____

_____

Some memorable events in your first three or four years were _____

_____

_____

_____

_____

Some of your strong personality traits that we noticed early _____

_____

_____

_____

· Manners ·
A child should always say what's
true
and speak when he is spoken to,
and behave mannerly at
table,
at least as far as he is able.

· FOR KAREL ·

Off to School

Your first school was _____

Your first teacher was _____

How you handled the idea of going to school _____
_____
_____
_____

On your very first day of school _____
_____
_____
_____
_____

After I left you on that first day, I felt _____
_____
_____
_____
_____

After your first day, you told me _____
_____
_____
_____

Your teacher told me _____
_____
_____
_____

At that age, you said that when you grew up, you wanted to be _____
_____
_____
_____
_____

HOME

IS WHERE ONE STARTS FROM

T.S. ELIOT

Primary School Years

The name of your primary school was _____

Your favorite activities during this time included _____

_____

_____

_____

Some of my favorite memories of you from this period were _____

_____

_____

_____

We were especially proud of you when _____

_____

_____

_____

Some additional comments about this time of your life _____

_____

_____

_____

_____

_____

_____

_____

Middle School and Junior High School Years

Your attitudes about school _____
_____

In your free time, you loved to _____
_____

During the summers, you _____
_____
_____

As you grew older, your personality really developed. My favorite things about you were _____
_____
_____
_____

Clothes you wore during this time _____
_____

I first started thinking of you as a "grown-up" when you _____
_____
_____

I was especially proud of you when _____
_____
_____

One time when you got into big trouble was _____
_____
_____
_____

High School Years

When you started high school, I remember that you were _____
_____
_____
_____

In high school you seemed especially interested in _____
_____
_____
_____

I was always impressed by your _____
_____
_____
_____

Some special memories I have from this time in your life are _____
_____
_____
_____

When you first started dating, I felt _____
_____
_____
_____

Something you did that you didn't think that I knew about _____
_____
_____
_____

Once you got into trouble for _____

_____

_____

_____

_____

You liked to talk about becoming a(n) _____

_____

_____

_____

_____

You were sometimes worried about _____

_____

_____

_____

_____

_____

After high school, you planned _____

_____

_____

_____

_____

_____

On your graduation day, I felt _____

_____

_____

_____

THERE IS ALWAYS ONE MOMENT
IN CHILDHOOD WHEN THE DOOR
OPENS AND LETS THE FUTURE IN.
— GRAHAM GREENE

See How You've Grown!

Photographs of you, as you've grown throughout the years, bring back special memories.

Here are some of my favorite photos along with my recollections

about the times when they were taken.

Family Memories

As a child, one thing you loved to do more than any other was _____

_____

_____

_____

_____

_____

_____

I hope if you have kids they're just like you in the way they _____

_____

_____

_____

_____

_____

_____

_____

A gift we gave you that you seemed to like more than any others _____

_____

_____

_____

_____

_____

Some of your best Halloween costumes were _____

_____

_____

For Mother's Day, you once gave me _____

_____

_____

_____

_____

One Father's Day, you gave your dad _____

_____

_____

_____

_____

We still laugh about the time _____

_____

_____

_____

_____

At family gatherings you were always the one who _____

_____

_____

_____

_____

_____

_____

_____

_____

_____

_____

Vacations

Your first trip was to _____

_____

_____

As a traveler, you were _____

_____

_____

To keep you entertained in the car, we _____

_____

_____

Your first airplane flight was _____

_____

_____

One of our best trips was _____

_____

_____

_____

_____

_____

_____

Some misadventures we had while vacationing were _____

_____

_____

_____

Some other vacation memories I have are _____

_____

_____

_____

_____

_____

_____

_____

_____

_____

_____

_____

_____

_____

_____

_____

_____

_____

_____

_____

_____

_____

_____

_____

HOME IS WHERE THE HEART IS

MORNING NEWS 1984 ©

Thoughts I'd Like to Share

The guiding principles in my life are _____
_____
_____
_____
_____
_____
_____
_____

In dealing with others, I've learned _____
_____
_____
_____
_____
_____
_____
_____
_____

When I'm feeling down, I like to think about _____
_____
_____
_____
_____
_____
_____
_____

Something that is very important to me that you may not realize _____

_____

_____

_____

_____

_____

_____

_____

When I look at you today, and think back on your life _____

_____

_____

_____

_____

_____

_____

_____

_____

_____

What I've learned from you _____

_____

_____

_____

_____

_____

_____

_____

_____

You are very interesting to me as a person, because _____

_____

_____

_____

_____

_____

_____

My greatest hope for you is _____

_____

_____

_____

_____

_____

_____

If I could live my life over again, something that I might do differently _____

_____

_____

_____

_____

_____

_____

_____

_____

Something that my parents taught me that I would like to pass along to you _____

_____

_____

_____

_____

_____

_____

_____

_____

_____

_____

_____

_____

_____

Let's Start a New Tradition!

Sharing these stories and thinking about family members and close friends

who have surrounded your life has been rewarding, fun, and sometimes a little sad.

I hope that you will cherish and safeguard these memories as I have.

If you've enjoyed reading this journal,

you might want to keep a journal of your own memories—

of all life's triumphs and struggles and day-to-day miracles.

Pass it on to your own children some day.

I guarantee that you'll be glad you did.

With all the love in my heart,

_____

Keepsakes and Remembrances

(Place for souvenirs, photos, etc.)

Assorted Thoughts

I WANT TO LIVE
BY THE SIDE OF
THE ROAD

AND BE A FRIEND
TO MAN

CEASE TO ASK WHAT THE MORROW WILL BRING
AND SET DOWN AS GAIN EACH DAY THAT FORTUNE GRANTS